geeky dream♥ats geeky dream♥ats geeky dream♥ats geeky dream♥ats

I1047035

geeky dreamboats

geeky dreamboats

A CELEBRATION

by Lacey Soslow and
Sarah O'Brien

QUIRK BOOKS

PHILADELPHIA

Copyright © 2009 by Quirk Productions, Inc.

All rights reserved. No part of this book may be reproduced in any form without written permission from the publisher.

Library of Congress Cataloging in Publication Number: 2008939277

ISBN: 978-1-59474-332-0

Printed in Singapore

Typeset in Clarendon, Din Schrift, Minion, and Univers

Designed by Jenny Kraemer
Production management by John J. McGurk

Distributed in North America by Chronicle Books
680 Second Street
San Francisco, CA 94107

10 9 8 7 6 5 4 3 2 1

Quirk Books
215 Church Street
Philadelphia, PA 19106
www.quirkbooks.com

table of contents

introduction: a tribute

DEAR ADORING FANS,

This is our gift to you. A book full of drool-inducing heartthrobs. No, there's no need to thank us, really. We saw the need for this book; we saw the countless tributes to the beauty of women. You know what we're talking about. Just take a look at your boyfriends' magazine collections. Go on, what do you see? *Maxim*, the Victoria's Secret catalog. Right. Now take a look at your magazines. Again, women all around. What gives? Where are all the men? We know. We hear you. And that is why you are holding *Geeky Dreamboats*. This can be your own little guilty pleasure. Don't be ashamed. We're here to tell you it's okay. You are not alone. There are scores of women out there who, like you, may have an unhealthy obsession with, say, Michael Cera.

We could have filled this book with sexy, unattainable men who are too perfect for words. The Brad Pitts and George Clooneys of the world. But let's face it, where's the fun in that? The thing with the geek is that he is within our grasp. He is attainable. At least we like to think so. See, we like a little geek in our objects of obsession. Who can fault us? The geeky man isn't arrogant, better dressed than us, or prone to scoping out every long-legged blonde who walks by. Sure, his bookshelves may be lined with *Star Wars* action figures, but rest assured, you'll never be worried that he's out picking up girls at the club.

We chose to celebrate the John Cusacks and the Andy Sambergs and the Adam Brodys of the bunch. So none of them may be the next

People's Sexiest Man Alive, but you'll notice they're smart (check out all the Ivy Leaguers!), funny (comedians galore!), and downright sweet (they eat Sunday dinners with their moms!). Yes, scores of them love video games, are vegetarians, love insects, play chess and Scrabble, took tap dancing lessons, and collect four-leaf clovers, but you know what? We love them even more because of it.

Sure, some of these cuties may appear a little dreamier than geeky or a little geekier than dreamy, but remember, the prevailing theme here is the beautiful and poetic combination that makes up the sexy nerd. Not everyone strikes that perfect balance, but we've found a slew of cuties who come pretty close, and we've ranked their appeal with our trusty Geekboat Meter. The Geekboat Meter ranks all the men, from the dreamy geeks with a few more pens in their pocket protector (Stephen Colbert) to the celeb nerds with personal trainers (Jake Gyllenhaal). And we've marked the quintessential geeky dreamboat poster boys (Michael Cera) with a kiss indicating who we think achieves that perfect balance of geeky dreaminess. You may not agree with all our selections, but we can assure you, you'll swoon, drool, and think some impure thoughts along the way!

So go ahead and ogle these men all you want. We've provided plenty of photos just for that purpose. Kick back and enjoy the eye candy, ladies, and let's pay tribute to these men who make us glad to be women.

IN MUTUAL ADORATION.
THE AUTHORS

Michael Cera

GEEKBOAT NUGGETS

BIRTHDAY: June 7, 1988

SIGN: Gemini

NATIONALITY: Canadian

PARENTS' NAMES: Luigi and Linda

SIBLINGS: An older sister Jordan and a younger sister Molly

FIRST CRUSH: Kelly Kapowski on *Saved by the Bell*

MOST MEMORABLE ROLES: George Michael Bluth in *Arrested Development*, Evan in *Superbad*, Paulie Bleeker in *Juno*

FUN FACT: Michael plays guitar in the band The Long Goodbye.

GEEKBOAT METER

WHY WE LOVE HIM

It might have been that time, in the second season of *Arrested Development* when he was sitting on Jason Bateman's lap. Or maybe it was when he was lathering his inner thighs with deodorant in *Juno*. Either way, Michael had us *way* before he said anything. Maybe it's those oversized khaki pants and festive print shirts, or the way he wears a sweatband and combs his side part. He's made many a woman in her twenties (and dare we say, thirties?) blush with girlish delight at his beauty and charm—and for that we love him.

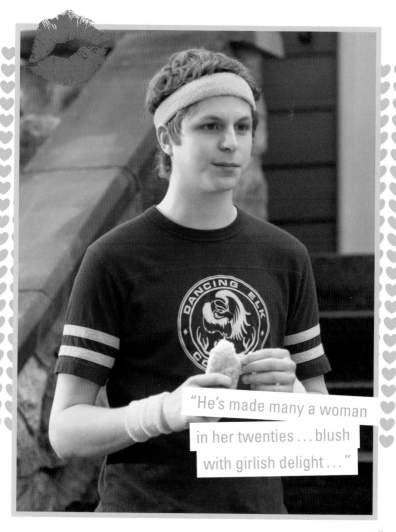

"He's made many a woman in her twenties ... blush with girlish delight ..."

Ryan Gosling

GEEKBOAT **NUGGETS**

BIRTHDAY: November 12, 1980

SIGN: Scorpio

PETS: A dog name George that he rescued from the pound

HOBBIES: Playing chess, reading, and playing the guitar and piano

FAVORITE MOVIE: *East of Eden*

SHOWBIZ START: Was a member of the Mickey Mouse Club alongside Christina Aguilera, Britney Spears, Justin Timberlake, JC Chasez, and Keri Russell

FUN FACT: As a child, Ryan's nickname was "Trouble" because he started fights in school.

GEEKBOAT **METER**

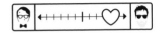

WHY WE **LOVE HIM**

Okay, so every girl between the ages of 8 and 88 swoons over Ryan. We get that. But he really has only himself to blame. He was the one who chose to star in *The Notebook* for godsakes! He is every woman's dream come true in that movie. Soon after its release Ryan became the golden boy of dreamboats everywhere, and we all regressed to boy-crazy thirteen-year-olds at the mere mention of his name. See, that's what happens when these men tug on women's heartstrings, so don't blame us for our girlish tendencies.

"He is every woman's dream come true . . ."

Paul Rudd

GEEKBOAT **NUGGETS**

BIRTHDAY: April 6, 1969

SIGN: Aries

FAVORITE T.V. SHOW: *LOST*

SCHOOLING: Majored in theater at the University of Kansas

COMMERCIAL WORK: Once starred in a commercial for Nintendo

FOOD DISLIKES: Hates condiments of any kind—ketchup, mayonnaise, and especially mustard

FUN FACT: Paul was a DJ at bar mitzvahs before his acting career took off.

WHY WE **LOVE HIM**

Paul is taking the world of comedy by storm, and we like it. As the irresistible Brian Fantana in *Anchorman*, he introduced us all to the power of Sex Panther, which he wore proudly and with enthusiasm. But it's not just the Casanovas that he can play. Oh, no. As bitter David in *The 40-Year-Old Virgin* and the emasculated Pete in *Knocked Up*, Paul stole the spotlight and left us enamored. Although he often plays second fiddle to comic leads, in our eyes, Paul is second fiddle to no one.

" ...Paul stole the spotlight and left us enamored."

Tobey Maguire

GEEKBOAT **NUGGETS**

BIRTHDAY: June 27, 1975

SIGN: Cancer

REAL NAME: Tobias Vincent Maguire

CLEAN LIVING: Practices yoga and is a vegetarian

COOKING ASPIRATIONS: Originally wanted to be a chef

VIDEO GAMER: Favorite games include Grand Theft Auto, Dead to Rights, and Lord of the Rings

POKER ACE: Won first prize ($95,480) at the Phil Helmuth Poker Invitational

FUN FACT: Tobey enjoys playing chess.

GEEKBOAT **METER**

WHY WE **LOVE HIM**

When Tobey was cast as Peter Parker in *Spider-Man*, he surprised us all by beefing up for the part. Somewhere, somehow, he got a six-pack. Not that we mind or anything. But despite his superhero role, he could still play the nerdy Peter Parker with such ease that we suspected the part didn't require much "acting." It's okay though, because any man who can embody both a geek and a superhero without skipping a beat can tie us up in his web any day of the week.

" ...he can tie us up in his web any day of the week."

HENRY WADSWORTH LONGFELLOW

Jemaine Clement & Bret McKenzie

(Flight of the Conchords)

JEMAINE

BIRTHDAY: January 10, 1974

SIGN: Capricorn

FUN FACT: Jemaine describes his fashion sense as "Prince, but when he's just going to the store or something—casual Prince."

BRET,

BIRTHDAY: June 29, 1976

SIGN: Cancer

BAND MAN: Played keyboard in the band The Black Seeds

FUN FACT: Bret has his own Topps trading card in the *Lord of the Rings* series.

WHY WE **LOVE THEM**

What's better than one nerdy sexpot? Why, two, of course. Oh, yes, we totally get why Mel is always stalking them. We would too if we lived in Brooklyn. They're poetic and lyrical, unafraid to show their emotions. Bret makes sweatshirts with animal prints hot and Jemaine wears sideburns well and knows just the time and place to sport a leather suit (it's not a look everyone can pull off). It's as if these boys are opposite sides to the same beautiful, shiny coin. We'd like to hold onto that dreamy coin for dear, dear life.

GEEKBOAT METER

Nick Swardson

GEEKBOAT **NUGGETS**

BIRTHDAY: October 9, 1976

SIGN: Libra

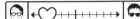

GEEKBOAT **METER**

MIDWEST BOY: Originally from Minneapolis, Minnesota

COMIC IDOLS: Bill Burr, Arj Barker, and Daniel Tosh

FAVORITE T.V. SHOWS: *Cheers*, *Three's Company*, and *The Jeffersons*

FIRST ROLE: A crazy David Bowie fan in *Almost Famous*

FUN FACT: Nick is the youngest comedian to get a Comedy Central special.

WHY WE **LOVE HIM**

We can't actually remember the first time we realized Nick was a bona fide dreamboat. It could have been when we heard about the prank he played on Jamie Kennedy. We laughed so hard, we actually peed our pants a little. So you can imagine our delight when he started showing up in movies. His role as Jon Heder's creepy stalker in *Blades of Glory* might have been overlooked for an Oscar, but it was not overlooked by our adoring eyes.

" ...it was not overlooked
by our adoring eyes."

Jonas Brothers

NICK JONAS

BIRTHDAY: September 16, 1992

SIGN: Virgo

FAVORITE SUBJECT: Spelling

FUN FACT: Nick owns 12 guitars.

JOE JONAS

BIRTHDAY: August 15, 1989

SIGN: Leo

FAVORITE SUBJECT: Math

FUN FACT: Joe's favorite sandwich is chicken cutlet with mayo.

KEVIN JONAS

BIRTHDAY: November 5, 1987

SIGN: Scorpio

FAVORITE SUBJECTS: Latin and History

FUN FACT: Kevin's favorite thing about himself is his hair.

WHY WE LOVE THEM

Okay, so maybe it's creepy that we sometimes watch their music videos alone in the dark, but we don't want to second-guess this love either! They have bouncy hair, dreamy ascots, and pants so tight, well we can't even say. Plus, we think their talent is totally underappreciated. People claim they're this "teen" bubblegum pop group, but their music has more depth and soul than so many mature musicians. So, believe us when we say, we will always be true to their art.

GEEKBOAT METER

♥21

Luke & Owen Wilson

LUKE

BIRTHDAY: September 21, 1971

SIGN: Virgo

NICKNAME: One-Take Wilson

FUN FACT: Luke attended high school at St. Mark's School of Texas, where he still holds the all-time record for the top five finishes in the 400- and 800-meter races.

OWEN

BIRTHDAY: November 18, 1968

SIGN: Scorpio

NICKNAME: "O"

MIDDLE NAME: Owen, Luke, and their other brother Andrew all have the same middle name: Cunningham.

FUN FACT: Owen is a fan of poetry and has been known to recite verses by famous poets.

WHY WE **LOVE THEM**

Actor brothers. Does it get any better than that? It's like asking if you prefer Rocky Road or Chocolate Chip Cookie Dough ice cream. Who can choose? Who cares?! We would take either of them in a heartbeat. Their quirky, one-of-a-kind roles in *The Royal Tenenbaums, Old School, The Darjeeling Limited, Wedding Crashers, Anchorman,* and *Rushmore* made them gods among men. So if we're ever down in Texas and happen to run into their mom and dad, we'll be sure to thank them for their fabulous genes.

GEEKBOAT METER

Zac Efron

BIRTHDAY: October 18, 1987

SIGN: Libra

FAVORITE MOVIE: *The Goonies*

FIRST CRUSH: Tyra Banks

FEARS: Sharks, zombies, and the girl from *The Ring*

FIRST CONCERT: Wallflowers

MOST PRIZED POSSESSION: Autographed baseball card collection

FUN FACT: Zac is very ticklish, especially under his arms.

GEEKBOAT **METER**

WHY WE **LOVE HIM**

We realize you're probably thinking, "Zac's not a geek!" But when you think about it, Zac is among the truest geeks of all. For starters, he sings and dances in a Disney musical franchise! Does it get any geekier than that? Nope. Plus, he clearly self-tans, plucks his eyebrows, and has highlighted hair. Yes, all this maintenance makes him dreamy, but seriously, it's beyond geeky. He's so clean cut that until he overdoses at the Chateau Marmont or has a sex scandal with a foxy cougar (hint, hint), we're keeping him around.

" ...Zac is among the truest geeks of all."

Zach Braff

BIRTHDAY: April 6, 1975

SIGN: Aries

HOMETOWN: South Orange, New Jersey

FAVORITE CEREAL: Life

FAVORITE T.V. SHOW: *LOST*

DIRECTOR: Directed the music video for Gavin DeGraw's "Chariot"

NICKNAME: Chicken Little

FUN FACT: Zach was the voice of the puppy in the Cottonelle T.V. commercials.

GEEKBOAT **METER**

WHY WE **LOVE HIM**

Zach ushered geekiness into the mainstream with *Garden State*, the film that brought attention to all the angsty tribulations of our twenties. Zach made us ponder how hard it is to be aloof, confused, and mysterious. And, after watching it, we couldn't help but feel (and fall) for him and his geeky, indie ways. Let's be honest, he made it cool to be geeky. And who doesn't love his tussled hair and goofball ways on *Scrubs*? Besides, the fact that he's just another Jewish boy from Jersey is another reason he belongs on this list.

" ...he made it cool to be geeky."

Mos Def

GEEKBOAT **NUGGETS**

BIRTHDAY: December 11, 1973

SIGN: Sagittarius

HOMETOWN: Brooklyn, New York

WHAT'S IN A NAME: Mos Def stands for "most definitely."

NICKNAMES: Pretty Flaco and The Mighty Mos Def

EATING HABITS: Vegetarian

EARLY BEGINNINGS: Started rapping when he was just 9 years old

FUN FACT: Mos Def adopted a British accent for his role in
  The Hitchhiker's Guide to the Galaxy.

GEEKBOAT **METER**

WHY WE **LOVE HIM**

A rapper with a heart of gold? A poet with an edge? Either way, Mos Def is *most definitely* dreamy. With that adorable baby face and social consciousness (hello, vegetarian!), Mos Def totally rocks that sensitive artist angle. And he's got celeb cred too! Mos appeared on *Chapelle's Show* and starred in *The Italian Job* as well as *Be Kind Rewind*, to name just a few. He's sensitive, shy, and those dimples, well, we'd ditch our carnivore ways for a glimpse of those dimples any day!

" ... Mos Def is *most definitely* dreamy."

John Cusack

BIRTHDAY: June 28, 1966

SIGN: Cancer

HOMETOWN: Chicago, Illinois

FAVORITE SPORTS TEAM: Chicago Cubs

HONORABLE MENTION: Is the subject of the song "Honorable Mention" by the band Fall Out Boy

FAVORITE FILM: *Apocalypse Now*

ROOMIES: Was once roommates with actor Jeremy Piven and is still close friends with him

FUN FACT: John's sister, actress Joan Cusak, has appeared in 16 of his movies.

GEEKBOAT **METER**

WHY WE **LOVE HIM**

We can sum this up in two words. *Say Anything*. John, in the trench coat, holding up the boombox, "In Your Eyes" blaring. You really can't top that. John plays the lovable Everyman role in movie after movie, from *Sixteen Candles* to *High Fidelity*, and every time he does, we flock to the theaters in droves. The thing is, there may be younger, newer, geekier dreamboats for each passing generation, but he is the original, the ultimate geeky dreamboat. And because of that, everyone will always fall short when compared to him.

"...he is the original, the ultimate geeky dreamboat."

Christopher Mintz-Plasse

GEEKBOAT **NUGGETS**

GEEKBOAT **METER**

BIRTHDAY: June 20, 1989

SIGN: Gemini

BIRTHPLACE: Los Angeles, California

FIRST GIG: Had no formal acting experience whatsoever prior to appearing in *Superbad*

NOMINATION: Was nominated in the category of Breakthrough Performance for his role in *Superbad* at the MTV Movie Awards

FUN FACT: Because he was only 17 when filming *Superbad*, Christopher had to have his mother present during his infamous sex scene.

WHY WE **LOVE HIM**

We have a confession to make: We didn't actually know who Christopher was before *Superbad*. Regardless, we're glad *Superbad* turned him into a household name, because McLovin' was the man in that movie, he was THE MAN. His nasally lisp, his joyride with the cops, his confidence and suaveness with the ladies . . . Let's face it, he stole the spotlight. The thing is, his geekiness reached epic proportions in that movie; but no worries, because McLovin' wore it well, he wore it WELL. And for that, we love him.

" . . . his geekiness reached epic proportions . . . "

Shia LaBeouf

GEEKBOAT NUGGETS

BIRTHDAY: June 11, 1986

SIGN: Gemini

PETS: Two bulldogs named Rex and Brando

IDEAL WOMAN: Likes dark, mysterious, Gothic-type girls

INSPIRATIONS: Jodie Foster, Jon Voight, Dustin Hoffman, and John Tuturo

MUSICAL INCLINATIONS: Plays the drums

FAMILY NAME: Was named after his grandfather who was a comedian

FUN FACT: Shia's name means "Thank God for the Beef."

GEEKBOAT METER

WHY WE LOVE HIM

We had our eye on Shia back when it was most likely illegal to have our eye on him. It seems that overnight he grew from a boy to a man, and we had to double-check that he was, in fact, legal. But there it is right there: He was born in 1986—1986! Lucky for us, we know how to embrace our inner cougars, and so we raced from *Transformers* to *Indiana Jones and the Kingdom of the Crystal Skull* just to get a glimpse of Shia's baby face, because, well, he makes us feel young again. And that is better than Botox any day.

"It seems that overnight
he grew from a
boy to a man ... "

Jon Stewart

BIRTHDAY: November 28, 1962

SIGN: Sagittarius

NICKNAMES: Lefty, Soupy, Poochy

CLASS BALLOT: Voted "Best Sense of Humor" by his high school class

PETS: A cat named Stan and two pit bulls named Shamsky and Monkey

FAVORITE MUSICIANS: Tom Waits, Bruce Springsteen, and Buffalo Tom

FUN FACT: Jon and his wife do the *New York Times* crossword every night. Jon actually proposed to her through a crossword puzzle.

GEEKBOAT **METER**

WHY WE **LOVE HIM**

Jonathan Stuart Leibowitz. That's his real name, and it's adorable! From playing soccer at William and Mary College to stocking shelves at Woolworth's to becoming a comedy rock star, he's proven himself to be a Renaissance man. He's almost as smart as he is funny, and we can't think of anything dreamier. Who else would we tune into every night to watch the fake news? Well, maybe Stephen Colbert, but he learned from the best!

"...he's proven himself to be a Renaissance man."

Kenan Thompson

GEEKBOAT NUGGETS

BIRTHDAY: May 10, 1978

SIGN: Taurus

SPORTS LOYALTIES: Is an Atlanta Falcons fan

IMPRESSIONS: Bill Cosby, Maya Angelou, Flava Flav, Randy Jackson, Al Roker, Colin Powell, Aretha Franklin, Lil' Kim, Patti LaBelle

FIRST MOVIE ROLE: *D2: The Mighty Ducks*

AUTHOR: Wrote a short story for *Chicken Soup for the Kid's Soul*

OLD FRIENDS: Is still good friends with Kel Mitchell, his costar on their show *Kenan and Kel*

FUN FACT: Kenan's first acting gig was in a chicken commercial.

GEEKBOAT METER

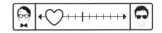

WHY WE LOVE HIM

We were so happy when Kenan joined the cast of *SNL* we may have done a little jig in midair. Kenan made us laugh till we cried (in a good way), and we knew it was only a matter of time before the world caught on to our little love affair with him. And what can we say? He plays a damn fine woman. He plays Star Jones better than she plays herself. Any man who can rock drag like Kenan deserves a nod in our book. So pardon the cliché, but he really is All That.

"He plays Star Jones better than she plays herself."

Jason Schwartzman

GEEKBOAT **NUGGETS**

BIRTHDAY: June 26, 1980

SIGN: Cancer

BAND ROOTS: Formed the band Phantom Planet when he was 14

FRIENDSHIPS: Is good friends with actress Claire Danes

PETS: Has a bulldog named Arrow and a cat named Extra Mayo

FUN FACT: Jason's mom is Talia Shire (Adrian of *Rocky* fame).

GEEKBOAT **METER**

WHY WE **LOVE HIM**

Not only did he star in our favorite movie ever—*Rushmore*—he is also a totally talented musician *and* a member of the super cool Coppola clan. It's true, Jason is not just a pretty face. We felt so proud when he broke free from his band Phantom Planet and took it up a notch with Coconut Records; his musical stylings surely have matured. From the beret-wearing Max Fischer to the goofy philosopher in *I ♥ Huckabees*, Jason melted our hearts, with some substance, no less.

"…Jason is not just a pretty face."

Demetri Martin

GEEKBOAT NUGGETS

BIRTHDAY: May 25, 1973

SIGN: Gemini

COLLEGE YEARS: Attended Yale University and NYU School of Law on full scholarship

HOBBIES: Skateboarding and constructing palindromes

INFLUENCES: Mitch Hedberg, Emo Phillips, Eddie Izzard, and Steven Wright

T.V. ROLE: Appeared as a keytar player named Demetri in the 2007 season finale of *Flight of the Conchords*

ALLERGY ALERT: Is allergic to peanuts

FUN FACT: Demetri can write with both hands at the same time.

GEEKBOAT METER

WHY WE LOVE HIM

From *The Daily Show* to *Flight of the Conchords* to his stand-up acts with his trusty easel, Demetri has earned his place in the comedic realm with his soothing monotone voice and geeky outfits. It's true that he has a passion for palindromes and is allergic to peanuts, two exceptionally geeky qualities that seal Demetri's fate as a comic nerd. But his tussled dark locks and deep chestnut eyes more than make up for it; so even though we live for PB&J sandwiches, we'd shun them for him any day!

42 ♥

" ...his tussled dark locks and deep chestnut eyes more than make up for it ..."

♥43

Jack McBrayer

BIRTHDAY: May 27, 1973

SIGN: Gemini

HOMETOWN: Macon, Georgia

COLLEGE YEARS: Studied theater management at the University of Evansville

LUCKY GUY: Collects four-leaf clovers

FIRST JOB: Worked at a pool-liner-manufacturing plant earning $4.25 an hour

FIRST BIG SCREEN ROLE: Glenn in *Talladega Nights*

FUN FACT: Jack was once chosen as employee of the month at Applebees.

GEEKBOAT METER

WHY WE LOVE HIM

As the endearing and ever-cheerful Kenneth in *30 Rock*, Jack is a refreshing breath of innocence that stands out in a world of cranky and sarcastic characters. With his Southern twang and straight moral compass, we can't help but be swept up in his world of sunshine and optimism. From honing his comedy craft at Second City in Chicago to cameos in goofy comedies like *Talladega Nights* and *Walk Hard* to the Mariah Carey video for "Touch My Body," he is a sweet, sweet shining star with major potential.

"...Jack is a refreshing breath of innocence..."

KENNETH

John Cho & Kal Penn

JOHN

BIRTHDAY: June 16, 1972

SIGN: Gemini

BIRTHPLACE: Seoul, South Korea

COLLEGE: Received a BA in literature from the University of California, Berkeley

FUN FACT: John starred in an episode of *The Family Feud* with his brothers.

KAL

BIRTHDAY: April 23, 1977

SIGN: Taurus

REAL NAME: Kalpen Suresh Modi

FUN FACT: Kal is a vegetarian and ate veggie burgers during the filming of *Harold and Kumar Go to White Castle.*

WHY WE **LOVE THEM**

Kalpen Suresh Modi, mmmm, it just rolls off the tongue. And sweet John Cho. Sure, some might think they're just the pretty faces from *Harold and Kumar Go to White Castle*, which is true, yes. But they'd be remiss to forget John and Kal's critically acclaimed work in the *American Pie* franchise (John!) and Van Wilder movies (Kal!). Ah, all those hormones and teen angst, it's no wonder those boys got mixed up with marijuana. But who can blame them? We'd gladly join them on a trip to White Castle any day!

GEEKBOAT METER

Martin Starr

GEEKBOAT NUGGETS

BIRTHDAY: July 30, 1982

SIGN: Cancer

BIRTHPLACE: Santa Monica, California

EDUCATION: Attended the Los Angeles School of the Performing Arts

FAMOUS MOM: Son of actress Jean St. James

ACTIVITIES: Enjoys swimming, bike riding, tennis, basketball, and soccer

MOST NOTABLE ROLE: Bill Haverchuck in *Freaks and Geeks*

FUN FACT: Martin has done commercials for Tropicana, Levis, and McDonald's

GEEKBOAT METER

WHY WE LOVE HIM

He rose to fame on *Freaks and Geeks* (that really should sum it up), but he's become so much more. It was an underrated show for sure, and although Martin made the cut purely based on Bill Haverchuck's oddly dreamy ways, he's recently risen among the ranks of Judd Apatow's crew. From the weird dude who didn't shave his beard in *Knocked Up* to popping up in other ensemble comedies like *Superbad*, we're not surprised this geeky star is rising. We sure do hope to see more of that goofy, handsome face!

" ...we're not surprised that this geeky star is rising."

Wes Anderson

GEEKBOAT **NUGGETS**

GEEKBOAT METER

BIRTHDAY: May 1, 1969

SIGN: Taurus

FULL NAME: Wesley Wales Anderson

EDUCATION: Studied philosophy at University of Texas

LITERARY INFLUENCES: F. Scott Fitzgerald and J. D. Salinger

IN THE FAMILY: Wes's brother does all the art and designs all the sets for Wes's movies.

FIRST FULL-LENGTH FEATURE: *Bottle Rocket*

FUN FACT: Wes and Owen Wilson were roommates at the University of Texas.

WHY WE **LOVE HIM**

Tall, check. Skinny, check. Fabulous glasses, check. Living film auteur, check. Okay, there you have it. Wes is a living legend among geeky dreamboats. He brought Bill Murray back to godlike status, his characters' costumes are Halloween fodder for years to come, and his movies make us laugh, cry, and even think. Plus his lifelong friendship with the Wilson brothers certainly works in his favor! A movie set with him, Owen, Luke, and Jason Schwartzman is a geeky dreamboat overload! Be still our beating hearts!

"Wes is a living legend among geeky dreamboats."

Mark Ruffalo

GEEKBOAT **NUGGETS**

BIRTHDAY: November 22, 1967

SIGN: Sagittarius

BIRTHPLACE: Kenosha, Wisconsin

ETHNICITY: Italian American

ATHLETE: Was on the wrestling team in high school

DREAM ROLE: Said that he would like to act in a Western film

DEDICATION: Has been to nearly 800 auditions

FUN FACT: When he first proposed to his wife, she turned him down. She accepted his second proposal two years later.

GEEKBOAT **METER**

WHY WE **LOVE HIM**

His soft-spoken ways, curly locks, and dark brown eyes draw us in so deeply, we sometimes forget our names. He has played a badass cop, geeky technician, and leading man, all without skipping a beat. When we read that he went to 800 auditions before landing a decent part and that his wife turned down his first marriage proposal, we just about launched a protest in his honor. Seriously, what is the matter with people? How much rejection can one man take? For the record, we never would have rejected this geeky dreamboat!

"His soft-spoken ways, curly locks, and dark brown eyes draw us in so deeply ..."

Jeremy Davies

GEEKBOAT NUGGETS

BIRTHDAY: October 8, 1969

SIGN: Libra

HOMETOWN: Traverse City, Michigan

REAL LAST NAME: Boring

FAMOUS DAD: Children's author Mel Boring

LEADING LADIES: Dated Drew Barrymore and Milla Jovovich

EARLY YEARS: Appeared in two episodes of *The Wonder Years*

FUN FACT: Jeremy lost 33 pounds to star in *Rescue Dawn* with Christian Bale.

GEEKBOAT METER

WHY WE LOVE HIM

It's safe to say that you're hot stuff when you have ex-girlfriends including Drew Barrymore and Milla Jovovich, but when your dreaminess is coupled with the total nerd-dom that comes along with the task of dazzling hearts and minds as the absent-minded physicist on *LOST*, well, you know you've achieved geeky dream-boat status. Jeremy's geeky vest, scruffy beard, and ill-fitting skinny tie are enough to put us over the edge. We'd love to be trapped on a tropical island with this nerdy professor!

"We'd love to be trapped on a tropical island with this nerdy professor!"

Jason Bateman

GEEKBOAT NUGGETS

BIRTHDAY: January 14, 1969

SIGN: Capricorn

MIDDLE NAME: Kent

FIRST GIG: Got into acting when, at age 10, he followed a friend to an audition for a role in an educational film and the director asked him to read for the lead

SPORTS FANATIC: Is an L.A. Dodgers fan

IN THE FAMILY: Jason's sister is actress Justine Bateman of *Family Ties* fame.

FUN FACT: Jason says, "I have a tendency to evolve into William Shatner, with my big fat face."

GEEKBOAT METER

WHY WE LOVE HIM

When he first burst onto the small screen in the 1980s as the hunky older brother on *The Hogans*, Jason was just a boy. When he resurfaced years later on *Arrested Development*, it was clear that he had grown into a TV DILF. He brought the geeky hotness as a bumbling single dad with a nutty family trying to hold everything together. Some of us even think that he outshined—dare we say?—Michael Cera. Younger doesn't necessarily mean better because, like a fine wine, this is one geeky dreamboat that gets better with age.

"He brought the geeky hotness ..."

Topher Grace

GEEKBOAT NUGGETS

BIRTHDAY: July 12, 1978

SIGN: Cancer

MUSICAL INTERESTS: Is a fan of Barry White

LEADING LADY: Dated Ivanka Trump

FAVORITE SPORTS: Tennis and Soccer

FAVORITE T.V. SHOW: *Mr. Show*

SMALL WORLD: Actress Chloë Sevigny often babysat Topher
when he was a child.

FUN FACT: Topher has a collection of baseball caps.

GEEKBOAT METER

WHY WE LOVE HIM

Although Ashton may get all the attention, our hearts belong to
Topher, in his tight corduroy pants, shaggy hairdo, and all his '70s
glory. There is just something about a man with a bony frame that
screams, "Feed me all your love and affection!" And although Topher
left the show and went on to bigger and better things, such as playing
the villain Venom in *Spider-Man 3*, in our minds, he'll always be our
scrawny '70s dreamboat.

" ...he'll always be our scrawny '70s dreamboat."

Jake Gyllenhaal

GEEKBOAT NUGGETS

BIRTHDAY: December 19, 1980

SIGN: Sagittarius

NOBLE BLOOD: Is a Swedish nobleman by birthright and his name appears in the Swedish *Almanac of Nobility*

DOG LOVER: Has two dogs, Boo and Atticus, that are named after characters in Jake's favorite book, *To Kill a Mockingbird*

MUSICAL CLASSMATES: Went to school with the musicians from Maroon Five

ROLE DEDICATION: Gained five pounds of muscle for his role in the film *Jarhead*

FUN FACT: Jake had his bar mitzvah party at a homeless shelter.

GEEKBOAT METER

WHY WE LOVE HIM

We could make a *Brokeback Mountain* joke here, but we'd like to think we're above that. The fact is Jake's acting career is diverse, and we salute him for that. He could have gone the teen movie route and taken on the easy heartthrob roles, but he didn't. He sought out more serious roles, and we noticed. We've also noticed that he's not a cad like a lot of other young actors. He's well-mannered, smart, adorable, and a true gentleman. He could quite possibly be the perfect man. Seriously, we really wish we knew how to quit him. Oops.

"He could quite possibly be the perfect man."

Rivers Cuomo

GEEKBOAT NUGGETS

BIRTHDAY: June 13, 1970

SIGN: Gemini

CHILDHOOD NICKNAME: Weezer

NAME ORIGIN: Was named Rivers because he was born near a river in New York and his mother liked the sound of the running water

BRAINIAC: Graduated Phi Beta Kappa from Harvard

FASHION STATEMENT: Is best known for his horn-rimmed glasses and his lightning-bolt guitar strap

MUSICAL INFLUENCES: Pixies, Stevie Ray Vaughan, Kiss, Nirvana, Lou Barlow, Giacomo Puccini, and Brian Wilson

FUN FACT: Rivers was raised on an ashram run by a yoga master.

GEEKBOAT METER

WHY WE LOVE HIM

Being the frontman of Weezer catapults Rivers to geek legend right off the bat, but there's so much more to his geek status than his alternative rock roots. For instance, he likes to play foosball, used to post on his own band's fan sites, and clearly has an Asian fetish. These are all the markings of a tried-and-true geeky dreamboat, not to mention the adorable horn-rimmed glasses. So, we'll just sit in our bedrooms and play the Buddy Holly song over and over again, wishing it was 1994 and we were Mary Tyler Moore.

"...there's so much more to his geek status than his alternative rock roots."

Michael Ian Black

GEEKBOAT NUGGETS

BIRTHDAY: August 12, 1971

SIGN: Leo

EDUCATION: Attended NYU, Tisch School

REAL NAME: Michael Schwartz

MTV DAYS: Starred in the MTV comedy troupe *The State*

WORDSMITH: Enjoys playing Scrabble

POKER PLAYER: Is a poker enthusiast who has appeared many times on *Celebrity Poker Showdown*

FUN FACT: Michael occasionally writes a column for *McSweeney's* entitled "Michael Ian Black Is a Very Famous Celebrity."

GEEKBOAT METER

WHY WE LOVE HIM

What's in a name? Is it the Michael, or the Ian, or the Black that gives us the tingles? Although he may have one pretentious name, he has the face of an angel and that indie smugness about him. And that face of an angel doesn't really age. He's looked the same since *The State*. And we should know, since we used to rush home on Friday nights to watch him, just him, on MTV. So, these days, we tune in to VH1's *Best Week Ever* because seeing Michael Ian Black's face leaves us all feeling like we truly have had the best week ever.

"…he has the face of an angel and that indie smugness about him."

Seth Meyers

GEEKBOAT NUGGETS

BIRTHDAY: December 28, 1973

SIGN: Capricorn

SPLIT LOYALTIES: Is a fan of both the Pittsburgh Steelers and the Boston Red Sox

COLLEGE DAYS: Graduated from Northwestern University

IMPERSONATIONS: Has done impersonations of John Kerry, Brian Williams, Michael Caine, Prince Charles, Peyton Manning, Ryan Seacrest, Sean Penn, Stone Phillips, Anderson Cooper, Tobey Maguire, Ty Pennington, and Carrot Top

POKER PLAYER: Won Bravo's Celebrity Poker Showdown tournament

FUN FACT: After graduating from college, Seth joined a traveling troupe group called Boom Chicago.

GEEKBOAT METER

WHY WE LOVE HIM

His boyish good looks, ear-to-ear grin, and spot-on impressions keep us tuning in to *SNL* every week. We're glad Tina Fey got the H-E-double-hockey-sticks off *SNL* so that he could take over Weekend Update. If Seth anchored all the nightly news channels, we'd be news junkies for sure! Not to mention we heard he donated his Celebrity Poker Showdown winnings to charity. A philanthropic geeky dreamboat? As our grandmas would say, "What a catch!"

"His boyish good looks...
keep us tuning in
to SNL every week."

Simon Pegg

BIRTHDAY: February 14, 1970

SIGN: Aquarius

X FACTOR: Is a big fan of *The X-Files*

PETS: Has a miniature Schnauzer named Minnie

GARAGE BAND: Was in a band called God's Third Leg when he was 16

THE GODFATHER: Is godfather to Chris Martin and Gwyneth Paltrow's daughter Apple

FUN FACT: Simon is a big *Star Wars* fan and his movies often include references to the franchise.

GEEKBOAT METER

WHY WE LOVE HIM

He fights zombies! And zombie killers are rad! Simon is like a big zombie-fighting teddy bear that makes us laugh in a time of crisis. The fact that he loves *Star Wars*, *The X-Files*, and zombies may make him the poster child of geeks, but he's still a dreamboat. When we watched *Shaun of the Dead*, we realized that when zombies take over the world, there's no one we'd rather have defending us than Simon Pegg. On top of all that, he has the one quality that blinds all women—a British accent.

"Simon is like a big zombie-fighting teddy bear . . ."

Adam Brody

GEEKBOAT NUGGETS

BIRTHDAY: December 15, 1979

SIGN: Sagittarius

FAVORITE HOLIDAY: Halloween

FAVORITE FOOD: The "Matt Miller" sandwich at Canter's Deli in Los Angeles

FAVORITE T.V. SHOW: *The Daily Show*

FAVORITE SPORTS: Surfing and basketball

GEEKY INTERESTS: Is a big fan of X-Men

PET PEEVE: Top 40 Radio DJs

FUN FACT: Adam worked at Blockbuster before acting.

GEEKBOAT METER

WHY WE LOVE HIM

Adam Brody is the dreamboat who introduced a whole generation of teens to Death Cab for Cutie, Penguin polo shirts, and Converse sneakers. He reminded us that comic books and samurai films are cool, as are video games and graphic novels. His nerd domination transformed the tone of *The OC* from sexy, coke-laden parties to head-nodding indie rock shows. Is he the voice of a generation? Perhaps. Do we desperately miss his witty one-liners and subtle interjections of pop-culture minutiae? Definitely.

"His nerd domination transformed the tone of *The OC*..."

Daniel Radcliffe

GEEKBOAT NUGGETS

BIRTHDAY: July 23, 1989

SIGN: Leo

BIRTHPLACE: London, England

PETS: Two border terriers

MUSICAL TALENT: Plays bass guitar

FAVORITE FILM: *12 Angry Men*

FUN FACT: Daniel likes to play pranks. He took costar Robbie Coltrane's cellular phone and changed it so all the messages were in Turkish.

GEEKBOAT METER

WHY WE LOVE HIM

When we first saw him, we couldn't resist those horn-rimmed, geeky glasses. Dudes with glasses set our hearts aflutter. And then, suddenly, he was over Harry Potter and performing in weird plays where he was in love with a horse. Kind of creepy. He was also naked on stage at age 17, also kind of creepy. But we love his appreciation of the arts. So, we'll ignore his creepy artistic endeavors and just remember him as the wholesome Harry Potter who cast a spell on us.

"Dudes with glasses set our hearts aflutter."

Barry Obama

GEEKBOAT NUGGETS

BIRTHDAY: August 4, 1961

SIGN: Leo

BIRTHPLACE: Hawaii

WHAT'S IN A NAME: Barack means "blessed" in Swahili.

FAVORITE CHILDREN'S BOOK: *Where the Wild Things Are*

FUN AND GAMES: Enjoys Scrabble

CHI-TOWN MAN: Is a Chicago White Sox and Chicago Bears fan

FUN FACT: In his spare time, Barack loves to cook chili, shoot hoops, and play poker.

GEEKBOAT METER

WHY WE LOVE HIM

Maybe it was his smile. Maybe it was his ears. Maybe it was the devilish way he said "sweetie" that put us into a swoon—or maybe it was just the impeccable grooming of the closet metrosexual that left us in shock and awe. Whatever it was, Barry had us from the first "yes we can." Obama Girl better watch out: She may have the bikini, but we've got the power to get out the vote. Could we spend the next eight years delighting in Barry's every press conference? Hanging on every word of his State of the Union? Yes. Yes, we can.

"...Barry had us from the first 'yes we can.'"

Matthew Broderick

GEEKBOAT NUGGETS

BIRTHDAY: March 21, 1962

SIGN: Aries

HOBBIES: Bowling, ping pong, and paddle ball

FAVORITE ACTORS: Dustin Hoffman, Robert De Niro, and Bill Murray

SOUTHPAW: Is left-handed

FUN FACT: Matthew ate dinner with his mother at her house every Sunday night (even after he got married) from 1981 until she died in 2003.

GEEKBOAT METER

WHY WE LOVE HIM

He defined cool for an entire generation. Anything that comes after is inevitably compared to the original movie that put Matthew on the map: *Ferris Bueller's Day Off*. Sure, he's had some notable hits since then, but he is forever etched in our brains as the adorably geeky Ferris. Not to mention, in real life, Matthew seems totally unaffected by Hollywood. He ate dinner with his mother every Sunday night for more than 20 years. Need we say more?

"He defined cool for an entire generation."

Pharrell Williams

GEEKBOAT **NUGGETS**

BIRTHDAY: April 5, 1973

SIGN: Aries

NICKNAMES: Pha-real, Lil' Skateboard P, P. Willy

FAVORITE ASTRONOMER: Carl Sagan

SCI-FI FAN: Enjoys the *Star Trek* series

WHAT'S IN A NAME: N*E*R*D stands for "No One Ever Really Dies"

BOARDER: Has a half-pipe in his house

FUN FACT: Pharrell was fired from three different McDonald's for being lazy.

GEEKBOAT **METER**

WHY WE **LOVE HIM**

From the brim of his trucker hat down to the bottoms of his Bapesters, Pharrell is the dreamiest N*E*R*D ever. Nobody rocks argyle sweaters and multiple cherub tattoos better than he does. We're wooed by his sweet falsetto and the ambient beats he lays down for rappers. We know that his "band" N*E*R*D is just a ruse to showcase his other nerdy hobbies of playing fancy guitars and skateboarding. No matter how many HP ink-jet-printer commercials he does, we know that his soul is still sensitive.

"We're wooed by his sweet falsetto ..."

Stephen Colbert

BIRTHDAY: May 13, 1964

SIGN: Taurus

ALL IN THE FAMILY: The youngest of eleven in an Irish Catholic family

SCI-FI FAN: Was a fan of science fiction and fantasy books as a child and cites the works of J. R. R. Tolkien among his favorites

UPRIGHT CITIZEN: Is a Sunday school teacher

FUN FACT: Stephen has his own Ben and Jerry's ice cream flavor— "Stephen Colbert's AmeriCone Dream."

GEEKBOAT **METER**

WHY WE **LOVE HIM**

We love Stephen as much as he loves Lady Liberty, and that's a lot. Back in the day, he melted our hearts as Chuck Noblet on *Strangers with Candy*; we swooned when he debated himself as a correspondent on *The Daily Show*; and he blew our minds at the White House Correspondents dinner. Now, *The Colbert Report* is our only source for news, ever. There's nothing hotter than a Peabody Award—except three Peabody Awards! Stephen Tyrone Colbert is truly The Greatest Living American. And that's because truthiness = sexiness.

"Stephen Tyrone Colbert is truly The Greatest Living American."

Kanye West

GEEKBOAT NUGGETS

BIRTHDAY: June 8, 1977

SIGN: Gemini

WHAT'S IN A NAME: *Kanye* means "only one" in Swahili

NICKNAMES: Ye, Konman

FAVORITE GAME: Connect 4

INFLUENCES: Erick Sermon, DJ Premier, Mase, A Tribe Called Quest, Nas, Run-DMC

FAVORITE BAND: Franz Ferdinand

FUN FACT: Kanye lived in China for a year as a child.

GEEKBOAT METER

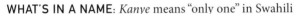

WHY WE LOVE HIM

We've known that Kanye was a shining star since his first album, when he rhymed, "I drink a Boost for breakfast and Ensure for dizzert. Somebody ordered pancakes, I just sip the sizzurp." Who else can boast about drinking Ensure and still be sexy?! Nobody else, that's who! And we know that fashion is Kanye's "first love" and his "true love," but we can dream. Maybe someday he will love us as much as he loves backpacks, Daft Punk, scarves, neon, and French techno.

"We've known that Kanye
was a shining star
since his first album ..."

Andy Samberg

BIRTHDAY: August 18, 1978

SIGN: Leo

REAL NAME: David Andrew Samberg

NICKNAME: Ardy

BIRTHPLACE: Berkeley, California

IMPERSONATIONS: Jack Johnson, David Blaine, Michael Sessions, Chuck Norris, Jimmy Fallon, and Dustin Diamond

FAVORITE DESSERT: Cupcakes

FUN FACT: Andy drives a black Lincoln Town Car.

GEEKBOAT METER

WHY WE LOVE HIM

We've pined after Andy since discovering the Lonely Island. At the very least, we want to be BFFs with him, binging on cupcakes and *The Chronicles of Narnia* together. His impersonations of Diablo Cody and a young Chuck Norris get us all steamy, and he brings a youthful silliness to the cast of *SNL*. We don't need diamond rings or fancy cars. All we need is an arts-and-crafts Christmas, Hanukkah, or Kwanzaa present where you (1.) Cut a hole in a box and (2.) Put your junk in that box . . .

"His impersonations of ... a young Chuck Norris get us all steamy ... "

Justin Long

GEEKBOAT NUGGETS

BIRTHDAY: June 2, 1978

SIGN: Gemini

HOMETOWN: Fairfield, Connecticut

CLASS BALLOT: Was voted "Most Likely Not to Be Seen in Class" in high school

PETS: Dog named Moose

LOOK ALIKE: Is commonly said to resemble actor Tim Allen

TITLE OF HIS ONE-MAN SHOW: "Justin Long: Dreams of a Douchebag"

FUN FACT: Justin appeared opposite Britney Spears in her movie debut, *Crossroads*.

GEEKBOAT METER

WHY WE LOVE HIM

We've got a crush on any fella who looks like a geeky hacker. Even though he claims to know nothing about computers, we can thank his parents for giving him the DNA of a hot computer programmer. His stint on *Ed* was short-lived, but it earned him a reputation as one fine nerd. He was such a natural as a failed cheerleader in *Dodgeball* and a hot and dangerous computer hacker in *Die Hard IV*. Clearly, the role of the anthropomorphized Mac computer in the Mac vs. PC commercials was made for Justin.

"...it earned him a reputation as one fine nerd."

Will Arnett

....

GEEKBOAT **NUGGETS**

BIRTHDAY: May 5, 1970

SIGN: Taurus

GEEKBOAT **METER**

TRADEMARK VOICE: Is known for his deep voice, which he has lent to voice-overs for Lamisil antifungal tablet commercials as well as for the character of Vlad, the bald eagle in *Horton Hears a Who*

ONLINE GAMER: Has admitted to being addicted to Xbox LIVE's Call of Duty and often plays with *The Office*'s John Krasinski and *SNL*'s Jason Sudeikis

MOST NOTABLE ROLE: Spoiled rich kid and failed magician George Oscar "Gob" Bluth II on *Arrested Development*

FUN FACT: Will's father was the CEO of Molson Breweries.

WHY WE **LOVE HIM**

That voice. That deep, raspy voice we'd recognize anywhere. We're glad Will started getting more roles after his role as Gob Bluth on *Arrested Development*, we just wish he would get more roles where we can actually *see* him. We appreciate that he's the voice behind several cartoon characters, but it's just a tease to hear him and not see his beautiful face!

"That voice. That deep, raspy voice we'd recognize anywhere."

Beck

BIRTHDAY: July 8, 1970

SIGN: Cancer

SCIENTOLOGY LEVEL: Sponsor for Total Freedom ($5,000+ donation)

WHAT'S IN A NAME: Took his mother's maiden name when his parents divorced

ALL IN THE FAMILY: Beck's grandfather, Al Hansen, is known for launching Yoko Ono's career.

BREAKTHROUGH SINGLE: "Loser"

FUN FACT: Beck's mother delivered Beck's wife, Marissa, and her twin brother, Giovanni Ribisi.

WHY WE **LOVE HIM**

Beck—Bek David Campbell—we crush on him for all the wrong reasons. We know he got that fancy name because his daddy was a Scientologist. He's had that dreamy, dazed Scientology glow ever since we've known him. And his monotone rapping and folksy crooning make *Odelay* a true pinnacle of Geekdom. We admit it: We're suckers for a scruffy haircut, an arty hat, and a killer robot walk.

"We're suckers for a scruffy haircut, an arty hat, and a killer robot walk."

Conan O'Brien

BIRTHDAY: April 18, 1963

SIGN: Aries

BIRTHPLACE: Brookline, Massachusetts

NICKNAMES: Coney, Consie, the Cone-Zone

HEIGHT: 6'4"

BRAINIAC: Graduated magna cum laude from Harvard University, with a BA in American history and literature

DANCING SHOES: Took tap dancing lessons as a child

FUN FACT: Conan's cousin is actor Denis Leary.

GEEKBOAT METER

WHY WE LOVE HIM

We've always enjoyed Conan's extra-springy orange hair, his lily-white pallor, and his sexy string-bean physique. He sure does stand out on a beach. And without those good looks he could never be a member of the crime-fighting Pale Force! It's true that he's popular in Finland because he bears a close resemblance to the first female President of Finland, Tarja Halonen. But hey, that lady is strikingly handsome. So, we'll let him pick us up in his forest green 1992 Ford Taurus anytime.

"We've always enjoyed Conan's ... sexy string-bean physique."

Sacha Baron Cohen

GEEKBOAT NUGGETS

BIRTHDAY: October 13, 1971

SIGN: Libra

INFLUENCES: Has said that Peter Sellers is his biggest influence

WRESTLING FANATIC: Has been a fan of professional wrestling his entire life

DANCING SHOES: Used to break-dance

FUN FACT: For the character of Borat, it took Sacha six weeks to grow in facial, body, and head hair.

GEEKBOAT METER

WHY WE LOVE HIM

What makes Sacha so awesome is the fact that he's downright hilarious, yet totally hot. He is the man behind Borat, the Kazakstani who wore a neon thong bikini, and that will forever seal his fate among the ranks of his fellow nerdy, hot men. Aside from being a comedic genius, he's also a genius genius, too. It's not like it's easy to weave cultural commentary and political humor into a mainstream movie. We can only hope that all his future characters have a similar affinity for tight bathing suit briefs!

" …he's downright hilarious, yet totally hot."

Elijah Wood

GEEKBOAT **NUGGETS**

BIRTHDAY: January 28, 1981

SIGN: Aquarius

NICKNAMES: Elwood and Monkey

FAVORITE BAND: Smashing Pumpkins

FAVORITE BOOKS: *The Hobbit* and *The Hunchback of Notre Dame*

MUSICALLY INCLINED: Plays the piano

INKED: Each of the nine *Fellowship of the Ring* actors got matching tattoos of the number 9 written in Elvish.

FUN FACT: Elijah was the first official member of the *Lord of the Rings* fan club.

GEEKBOAT **METER**

WHY WE **LOVE HIM**

Those piercing baby blues. Need we say more? Elijah grew up onscreen in front of us, maturing from successful child actor to respected adult actor with an impressive list of film credits a mile long. His rise to fame as Frodo Baggins in *Lord of the Rings* didn't go to his head, and when he said that "I think being different, being against the grain of society, is the greatest thing in the world," well, we just about scooped him up and put him in our pockets for safekeeping.

"Those piercing baby blues.

Need we say more?"

Edward Norton

GEEKBOAT NUGGETS

BIRTHDAY: August 18, 1969

SIGN: Leo

SPORTS FAN: Is a Baltimore Orioles fan

INKED: Has a Black Flag tattoo on his upper back

MULTILINGUAL SKILLS: Speaks French, Spanish, and Japanese

AVIATOR: Has a private pilot's license

BRAINIAC: Graduated from Yale

FUN FACT: Ed's father was an attorney for Jimmy Carter.

GEEKBOAT METER

WHY WE LOVE HIM

Ed is the thinking woman's crumpet. His movies make us use our heads, and thinking may equal geeky, but it also equals sexy. From *American History X* to *Fight Club*, *Rounders*, and everything in between, Ed proves that you can be smart and cute (contrary to what you thought in 7th grade). Sure, he's had a few cheesy roles (*The Hulk*, anyone?), but who hasn't? He may play the Hulk on-screen, but he'll always be the scrawny intellectual to us.

"Ed is the thinking woman's crumpet."

Dominic Monaghan

BIRTHDAY: December 8, 1976

SIGN: Sagittarius

BUG ENTHUSIAST: Loves insects and has a pet leaf-mantis and black widow spider

VIDEO GAMER: Enjoys video games and often hosts gaming parties at his house

FILM MEMENTO: Kept a pair of the Hobbit feet that he used in *Lord of the Rings*

FUN FACT: Dominic first auditioned for the role of Sawyer on *LOST*.

GEEKBOAT **METER**

WHY WE **LOVE HIM**

Dominic rose to fame as a hobbit in the *Lord of the Rings* trilogy, but when he took off his hobbit costume—and his shirt—in *LOST*, he *really* caught our attention as the troubled yet adorable Charlie who falls for Claire and befriends Hurley. That British accent and mischievous grin gets us every time, and the fact that Dominic's into nature, especially bugs, well that just about seals his fate as a geek worthy of our attention. Let's just say if we were lost on that island with him, we wouldn't be looking for a way off.

"That British accent and mischievous grin gets us every time . . . "

Seth Rogen

GEEKBOAT **NUGGETS**

BIRTHDAY: April 15, 1982

SIGN: Aries

EARLY DAYS: First stand-up experience, at age 13, was in a Vancouver gay bar

BIG BREAK: Was discovered by Judd Apatow, who cast him in his series *Freaks and Geeks*

COMEDY TIES: Worked for one season as a writer on Sacha Baron Cohen's *Da Ali G Show*

MOST NOTABLE MOVIE CREDITS: *Knocked Up*, *Superbad*, *The 40-Year-Old Virgin*, *Pineapple Express*

FUN FACT: Seth's parents met in Israel.

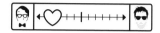

WHY WE **LOVE HIM**

As part of Judd Apatow's comedy crew, Seth has rightly earned his spot as part of this ensemble. Writing *Superbad* put him on the map, and in *Knocked Up* he proved to nerdy guys everywhere that yes, the nerd can get the hot girl. Plus, he's singlehandedly breathed new life into the bromances that have come to define such films as *The 40-Year-Old Virgin* and *Pineapple Express*. And what more could a girl ask for then to see not one, but two geeky dreamboats chumming together for a two-and-a-half-hour movie?

" ...he proved ...that yes,
the nerd can get
the hot girl."

Ira Glass

GEEKBOAT NUGGETS

BIRTHDAY: March 3, 1959

SIGN: Pisces

FIRST RADIO JOB: Writing jokes for Baltimore shock jock Johnny Walker

FAMILY TIES: Dad's first cousin is experimental composer Philip Glass

ANIMAL RIGHTS: Became a vegetarian after realizing chickens have distinct personalities

PET LOVER: Owns a pit bull

FUN FACT: Ira dated cartoonist Lynda Barry, becoming the inspiration for her story "Head Lice and My Worst Boyfriend."

GEEKBOAT METER

WHY WE LOVE HIM

Can a man named Ira have any other destiny than pure geekdom? When you've studied semiotics at Brown, wear Buddy Holly frames, and can lay claim to fame as the man who (sort of) discovered David Sedaris, there's just no point in denying: You've been marked for geeky greatness. We can listen to Ira's sexy, breathless, trip-over-his-words storytelling on NPR's *This American Life* for hours on end. Imitate him all you want, Ira-wannabes, but in the words of Donny and Marie, ain't nothing like the real thing, baby . . .

"Can a man named Ira have any other destiny than pure geekdom?"

Jimmy Fallon

GEEKBOAT NUGGETS

BIRTHDAY: September 19, 1974

SIGN: Virgo

AUTHOR: Cowrote *I Hate This Place: The Pessimist's Guide to Life* with his sister Gloria Fallon

SNL: Became a regular *Saturday Night Live* cast member in 1998, a lifelong dream

CLASS BALLOT: Was voted "Most Likely to Replace Dave Letterman" in elementary school

FUN FACT: Jimmy is close friends with actress Parker Posey, who was his neighbor in New York City.

GEEKBOAT METER

WHY WE LOVE HIM

As the bumbling, goofy cast member who always breaks character and bursts into laughter on *Saturday Night Live*, Jimmy captured our hearts from the first time he graced our TV screens. From his spot-on impressions of Adam Sandler to his wicked-awesome portrayal of a diehard Red Sox fan in *Fever Pitch*, Jimmy—with his disheveled hair and tortoiseshell glasses—redefines adorable geekiness and reminds us all of some long-forgotten geeky classmate from the seventh grade who always made us laugh.

" . . . he reminds us all of some long-forgotten geeky classmate . . . "

Michael Showalter

BIRTHDAY: June 17, 1970

SIGN: Gemini

NICKNAME: "Show"

HOMETOWN: Born and raised in Princeton, New Jersey

BRAINIAC: Graduated from Brown University

PETS: Has a cat named Lester

HOBBIES: Likes basketball and chess

FUN FACT: Michael's childhood dream was to be a cartoonist.

GEEKBOAT **METER**

WHY WE **LOVE HIM**

It's always those well-educated geeky Jewish boys who really get-cha! And everyone knows *The State* was the best show ever. During the mid-nineties we would tune in to MTV to catch a glimpse of apathetic Doug—how hilarious was it that Uncle Robert was Bob Dylan?—but we digress. Seriously, when Michael teamed up with Michael Ian Black (most notably of *Wet Hot American Summer* and *Stella* fame) it was like a sexy, geeky explosion! Hot + geeky + funny + smart is like super geeky dreamboat overload!

"Hot + geeky + funny + smart is like super geeky dreamboat overload!"

John Krasinski

GEEKBOAT NUGGETS

BIRTHDAY: October 20, 1979

SIGN: Libra

HOMETOWN: Boston, Massachusetts

FOOD LIKES/DISLIKES: Loves chocolate pudding but can't stand JELL-O

VIDEO GAME FUN: Often plays video games on set with his cast mates of *The Office*

SIDE JOB: Was once a bartender in Manhattan

FIRST GIG: Interned at *Late Night with Conan O'Brien*

FUN FACT: John can juggle.

GEEKBOAT METER

WHY WE LOVE HIM

John's portrayal of Jim on *The Office* turned us into giggly little schoolgirls who wrote his name in hearts on our notebooks. He reminds us of our eighth grade crush, that nice boy who sat across from us in Pre-Algebra and shared his fruit roll-up with us. You could actually hear our hearts break when he left for the Stamford branch. We yelled dirty words at the T.V. and threatened to stop watching *The Office* altogether if John didn't come back. But he did, and we were happy, and all was at peace with the world.

"John ... turned us into giggly little schoolgirls ... "

photo credits

All photos courtesy Everett Collection except Demetri Martin photo (page 43) courtesy Greg Cavic.

Cover: Michael Cera photo by Michael Germana; Bret McKenzie photo by Rob Rich; Jemaine Clement photo by Rob Rich; Adam Brody photo © WB.

Interior: Michael Cera photo TM & © Fox Searchlight, all rights reserved; Ryan Gosling photo © MGM; Paul Rudd photo © Universal; Tobey Maguire photo © Columbia; Bret McKenzie & Jemaine Clement photo by Nicole Rivelli/© HBO; Nick Swardson photo © Sony Pictures; Jonas Brothers photo by Kristin Callahan; Luke Wilson & Owen Wilson photo © Buena Vista Pictures; Zac Efron photo by Adam Larkey/© Disney Channel; Zach Braff photo by Mitch Haaseth/© NBC; Mos Def photo © Paramount; John Cusack photo © Warner Bros.; Christopher Mintz-Plasse photo © Columbia Pictures; Shia LaBeouf photo © Walt Disney; Jon Stewart photo by Norman Jean Roy/ © Comedy Central; Kenan Thompson photo © Screen Gems; Jason Schwartzman photo © Buena Vista Pictures; Jack McBrayer photo by Nicole Rivelli/© NBC; John Cho & Kal Penn photo © New Line; Martin Starr photo © Universal Pictures; Wes Anderson photo © Touchstone; Mark Ruffalo photo © Focus Features; Jeremy Davies photo © Gramercy Pictures; Jason Bateman photo © Weinstein Company; Topher Grace photo © DreamWorks; Jake Gyllenhaal photo © Newmarket Releasing; Rivers Cuomo photo by Alex Sudea/Rex USA; Michael Ian Black photo © NBC; Seth Meyers photo © NBC; Simon Pegg photo © Rogue Pictures; Adam Brody photo © Warner Independent; Daniel Radcliffe photo by Ray Burmiston/© HBO/BBC; Barack Obama photo by Ron Sachs/Rex USA; Matthew Broderick photo TM and © 20th Century Fox Film Corp., all rights reserved; Pharrell Williams photo by Jared Milgrim; Stephen Colbert photo by Joel Jeffries/© Comedy Central; Kanye West photo by Adam Orchon; Andy Samberg photo by Dee Cercone; Justin Long photo © Walt Disney; Will Arnett photo by Rob Rich; Beck photo by Alison Dyer; Conan O'Brien photo © NBC; Sacha Baron Cohen TM & © 20th Century Fox, all rights reserved; Elijah Wood photo by Michael Germana; Edward Norton photo © Universal; Dominic Monaghan photo © ABC/Mario Perez; Seth Rogen photo © Columbia Pictures; Ira Glass photo by Douglas Barnes/© Showtime; Jimmy Fallon photo by Katy Winn; Michael Showalter photo © IFC Films; John Krasinski photo © NBC.

geeky dreamboats